The Mixed Drinks Collection

Shooters

R&R Publishing

Introduction

METHODS OF MIXING COCKTAILS
The four methods below are the most common processes of mixing cocktails:-

1. Shake
2. Stir
3. Build
4. Blend

1. SHAKE: To shake is to mix a cocktail by shaking it in a cocktail shaker by hand. First, fill the glass part of the shaker three quarters full with ice, then pour the ingredients on top of the ice. Less expensive ingredients are more frequently poured before the deluxe ingredients. Pour the contents of the glass into the metal part of the shaker and shake vigorously for ten to fifteen seconds. Remove the glass section and using a Hawthorn strainer, strain contents into the cocktail glass. Shaking ingredients that do not mix easily with spirits is easy and practical (juices, egg whites, cream and sugar syrups).

Most shakers have two or three parts. In a busy bar, the cap is often temporarily misplaced. If this happens, a coaster or the inside palm of your hand is quite effective. American shakers are best.

To sample the cocktail before serving to the customer, pour a small amount into the shaker cap and using a straw check the taste.

2. STIR: To stir a cocktail is to mix the ingredients by stirring them with ice in a mixing glass and then straining them into a chilled cocktail glass. Short circular twirls are most preferred. (N.B. The glass part of the American shaker will do well for this.) Spirits, liqueurs and vermouths that blend easily together are mixed by this method.

3. BUILD: To build a cocktail is to mix the ingredients in the glass in which the cocktail is to be served, floating one on top of the other. Hi-Ball, long fruit juice and carbonated mixed cocktails are typically built using this technique. Where possible a swizzle stick should be put into the drink to mix the ingredients after being presented to the customer. Long straws are excellent substitutes when swizzle sticks are unavailable.

4. BLEND: To blend a cocktail is to mix the ingredients using an electric blender/mixer. It is recommended to add the fruit (fresh or tinned) first. Slicing small pieces gives a smoother texture than if you add the whole fruit. Next, pour the alcohol. Ice should always be added last. This order ensures that the fruit is blended freely with the alcoholic ingredients allowing the ice to gradually mix into the food and beverage, chilling the flavour. Ideally, the blender should be on for at least 20 seconds. Following this procedure will prevent ice and fruit lumps that then need to be strained.

If the blender starts to rattle and hum, ice may be obstructing the blades from spinning. Always check that the blender is clean before you start. Angostura Bitters is ammonia based which is suitable for cleaning. Fill 4 to 5 shakes with hot water, rinse and then wipe clean.

TECHNIQUES IN MAKING COCKTAILS

1. SHAKE AND POUR: After shaking the cocktail, pour the contents straight into the glass. When pouring into Hi-Ball glasses and sometimes old fashioned glasses the ice cubes are included. This eliminates straining.

2. SHAKE AND STRAIN: Using a Hawthorn strainer (or knife) this technique prevents the ice going into the glass. Straining protects the cocktail ensuring melted ice won't dilute the flavour and mixture.

3. FLOAT INGREDIENTS: Hold the spoon right way up and rest it with the lip slightly above the level of the last layer. Fill spoon gently and the contents will flow smoothly from all around the rim. Use the back of the spoons dish only if you are experienced.

4. FROSTING (sugar and salt rims): This technique is used to coat the rim of the glass with either salt or sugar. First, rub lemon/orange slice juice all the way around only the glass rim. Next, holding the glass by the stem upside down, rest on a plate containing salt or sugar and turn slightly so that it adheres to the glass. Pressing the glass too deeply into the salt or sugar often results in chunks sticking to the glass. A lemon slice is used for salt and an orange slice is used for sugar.

To achieve colour affects, put a small amount of grenadine or coloured liqueur in a plate and coat the rim of the glass, then gently place in the sugar. The grenadine absorbs the sugar and turns it pink. This is much easier than mixing grenadine with sugar and then trying to get it to stick to the glass.

HELPFUL HINTS
Cocktail mixing is an art which is expressed in the preparation and presentation of the cocktail.

HOW TO MAKE A BRANDY ALEXANDER CROSS
Take two short straws and, with a sharp knife, slice one of the straws half way through in the middle and wedge the other uncut straw into the cut straw to create a cross.

STORING FRUIT JUICES
Take a 750ml bottle and soak it in hot water to remove the label and sterilise the alcohol. The glass has excellent appeal and you'll find it easier to pour the correct measurement with an attached nip pourer.

SUGAR SYRUP RECIPE
Fill a cup or bowl (depending on how much you want to make) with white sugar, top it up with boiling water until the receptacle is just about full and keep stirring until the sugar is fully dissolved. Refrigerate when not in use. Putting a teaspoon of sugar into a cocktail is being lazy, it does not do the job properly as the sugar dissolves.

JUICE TIPS
Never leave juices, Coconut Cream or other ingredients in cans. Pour them into clean bottles, cap and refrigerate them. All recipes in this book have been tested with Berri fruit juices.

ICE
Ice is probably the most important part of cocktails. It is used in nearly all cocktails. Consequently ice must be clean and fresh at all times. The small squared cubes and flat chips of ice are superior for chilling and mixing cocktails. Ice cubes with holes are inefficient. Wet ice, ice scraps and broken ice should only be used in blenders.

Introduction

CRUSHED ICE

Take the required amount of ice and fold into a clean linen cloth. Although uncivilised, the most effective method is to smash it against the bar floor. Shattering with a bottle may break the bottle. Certain retailers sell portable ice crushers. Alternatively a blender may be used. Half fill with ice and then pour water into the blender until it reaches the level of the ice. Blend for about 30 seconds, strain out the water and you have perfectly crushed ice. Always try and use a metal scoop to collect the ice from the ice tray.

Never pick up the ice with your hands. This is unhygienic. Shovelling the glass into the ice tray to gather ice can also cause breakages and hence should be avoided where possible.

It is important that the ice tray is cleaned each day. As ice is colourless and odourless, many people assume wrongly it is always clean. Taking a cloth soaked in hot water, wipe the inside of the bucket warm. The blenders used for all of our bar requirements are Moulinex blenders with glass bowls. We have found these blenders to be of exceptional quality.

GLASSES

Cordial (Embassy):	30ml
Cordial (Lexington):	37ml
Tall Dutch Cordial:	45ml
Whisky Shot:	45ml
Martini Glass:	90ml
Cocktail Glass:	90ml, 140ml
Champagne Saucer:	140ml
Champagne Flute:	140ml, 180ml
Wine Goblet:	140ml, 190ml
Old Fashioned Spirit:	185ml, 210ml, 290ml
Fancy Cocktail:	210ml, 300ml
Fancy Hi-Ball Glass:	220ml, 350ml, 470ml
Hurricane Glass:	230ml, 440ml, 650ml
Irish Coffee Glass:	250ml
Margarita Glass:	260ml
Hi-Ball Glass:	270ml, 285ml, 330ml
Footed Hi-Ball Glass:	270ml, 300ml
Salud Grande Glass:	290ml
Fiesta Grande Glass:	350ml, 490ml
Poco Grande Glass:	380ml
Brandy Balloon:	650ml

A proven method to cleaning glasses is to hold each glass individually over a bucket of boiling water until the glass becomes steamy and then with a clean linen cloth rub in a circular way to ensure the glass is polished for the next serve

Cocktails can be poured into any glass but the better the glass the better the appearance of the cocktail.

One basic rule should apply and that is, use no coloured glasses as they spoil the appearance of cocktails. All glasses have been designed for a specific task, e.g.,

1. Hi-Ball glasses for long cool refreshing drinks.
2. Cocktail glasses for short sharp, or stronger drinks.
3. Champagne saucers for creamy after-dinner style drinks, etc.,

The stem of the glass has been designed so you may hold it whilst polishing, leaving the bowl free of marks and germs so that you may enjoy your drink. All cocktail glasses should be kept in a refrigerator or filled with ice while you are preparing the cocktails in order to chill the glass. An appealing affect on a 90ml cocktail glass can be achieved by running the glass under cold water and then placing it in the freezer.

GARNISHES AND JUICES

Banana	Onions
Celery	Oranges
Cucumber	Pineapple
Lemons	Red Maraschino Cherries
Limes	Rockmelon
Mint leaves	Strawberries
Olives	Canned fruit
Celery salt	Nutmeg
Chocolate flake	Pepper, Salt
Cinnamon	Tomato
Fresh eggs	Sugar and sugar cubes
Fresh single cream	Tabasco sauce
Fresh milk	Worcestershire sauce
Apple	Orange and Mango
Carbonated waters	Pineapple
Coconut Cream	Sugar syrup
Lemon – pure	Canned nectars
Orange	Canned pulps
Jelly Babies	Crushed Pineapple
Almonds	Blueberries
Apricot Conserve	Red Cocktail Onions
Vanilla Ice Cream	Flowers (assorted)

Simplicity is the most important fact to keep in mind when garnishing cocktails. Do not overdo the garnish; make it striking, but if you can't get near the cocktail to drink it then you have failed. Most world champion cocktails just have a lemon slice, or a single red cherry.

Tall refreshing Hi-Balls tend to have more garnish as the glass is larger. A swizzle stick should be served nearly always in long cocktails. Straws are always served for a lady, but optional for a man.

Plastic animals, umbrellas, fans and a whole variety of novelty goods are now available to garnish with, and they add a lot of fun to the drink.

ESSENTIAL EQUIPMENT FOR A COCKTAIL BAR

Cocktail shaker	Waiter's friend corkscrew
Hawthorn Strainer	Bottle openers
Mixing glass	Ice scoop
Spoon with muddler	Ice bucket
Moulinex Electric blender	Free pourers
Knife, cutting board	Swizzle sticks, straws
Measures (jiggers)	Coasters and napkins
Can opener	Scooper spoon (long teaspoon)
Hand cloths for cleaning glasses	

Introduction

Liqueurs

Advocaat	Galliano
Amaretto	Grand Marnier
Bailey's Irish Cream	Kahlúa
Benedictine	Kirsch
Blue Curacao	Lena Banana
Cassis	Mango
Chartreuse – Green	Midori
Chartreuse – Yellow	Peach
Cherry Advocaat	Pimm's
Cherry Brandy	Sambuca – di Galliano
Clayton's Tonic (Non-alcoholic)	Sambuca – Lago Nera
Cointreau	Sambuca – Opal Nera
Creme de Menthe Green	Sambuca – Romana
Dark Creme de Cacao	Strawberry
Drambuie	Tia Maria
Frangelico	

Vermouth

Cinzano Bianco Vermouth	Martini Bianco Vermouth
Cinzano Dry Vermouth	Martini Dry Vermouth
Cinzano Rosso Vermouth	Martini Rosso Vermouth

ESSENTIAL EQUIPMENT FOR A COCKTAIL BAR

Cocktail shaker	Waiter's friend corkscrew
Hawthorn Strainer	Bottle openers
Mixing glass	Ice scoop
Spoon with muddler	Ice bucket
Moulinex Electric blender	Free pourers
Knife, cutting board	Swizzle sticks, straws
Measures (jiggers)	Coasters and napkins
Can opener	Scooper spoon (long teaspoon)
Hand cloths for cleaning glasses	

DESCRIPTION OF LIQUEURS AND SPIRITS

Advocaat: A combination of fresh egg whites, yolks, sugar, brandy and spirit. Limited shelf life, Recommend shelf life 12-15 months from manufacture.

Amaretto: A rich subtle liqueur with a unique almond flavour.

Angostura Bitters: An essential part of any bar or kitchen. A unique additive whose origins date back to 1824. A mysterious blend of natural herbs and spices, both a seasoning and flavouring agent, in both sweet and savoury dishes and drinks. Ideal for dieters as it is low in sodium and calories.

Baileys Irish Cream: The largest selling liqueur in the world, was introduced onto the Australian market in 1974. It is a blend of Irish Whiskey, softened by Irish Cream and other flavourings. It is a natural product.

Benedictine: A perfect end to a perfect meal. Serve straight, with ice, soda, or as part of a favourite cocktail.

Bourbon – Rebel Yell: Has a deep flavour of one of America's authentic bourbon whiskies.

Brandy – Milne: Smooth and mild Australian spirit, is considered a very smooth and palatable brandy, ideal for mixing.

Campari: A drink for many occasions, both as a long or short drink, or as a key ingredient in many fashionable cocktails.

Cassis: Deep, rich purple promises and delivers a regal and robust flavour and aroma. Cassis lends itself to neat drinking or an endless array of delicious sauces and desserts.

Chartreuse: A liqueur available in either yellow or green colour. Made by the monks of the Carthusian order. The only world famous liqueur still made by monks.

Cherry Advocaat: Same as Advocaat, plus natural cherry flavours and colour is added.

Cherry Brandy: Is made from concentrated, morello cherry juice. Small quantity of bitter almonds and vanilla is added to make it more enjoyable as a neat drink before or after dinner. Excellent for mixers, topping, ice cream, fruit salads, pancakes, etc.

Coconut: A smooth liqueur, composed of exotic coconut, heightened with light-bodied white rum.

Cointreau: Made from a neutral grain spirit, as opposed to Cognac. An aromatic flavour of natural citrus fruits. A great mixer or delightful over ice.

Creme de Cacao Dark: Rich, deep chocolate. Smooth and classy. Serve on its own, or mix for all kinds of delectable treats.

Creme de Cacao White: This liqueur delivers a powerfully lively, full bodied chocolate flavour. Excellent ingredient when absence of colour is desired.

Creme de Grand Marnier: A blend of Grand Marnier and smooth French cream. A premium product, a very smooth taste with the orange/cognac flavour blending beautifully with smooth cream. Introduced to Australia in 1985.

Creme de Menthe Green: Clear peppermint flavour, reminiscent of a fresh, crisp, clean winter's day in the mountains. Excellent mixer, a necessity in the gourmet kitchen.

Creme de Menthe White: As Creme de Menthe Green, when colour is not desired.

Curacao Blue: Same as Triple Sec, brilliant blue colour is added to make some cocktails more exciting.

Curacao Orange: Again, same as above, but stronger in orange, colouring is used for other varieties of cocktail mixers.

Curacao Triple Sec: Based on natural citrus fruits. Well known fact is citrus fruits are the most important aromatic flavour constituents. Interesting to know citrus fruit was known 2,000 years before Christ. As a liqueur one of the most versatile. Can be enjoyed with or without ice as a neat drink, or used in mixed cocktails more than any other liqueur. Triple Sec – also known as White Curacao.

Introduction

Galliano: The distinguished taste! A classic liqueur that blends with a vast array of mixed drinks.

Gin – Gilbey's: The number one selling Gin in Australia. Its aroma comes from using the highest quality juniper berries and other rare and subtle herbs. Perfect mixer for both short and long drinks.

Kirsch: A fruit brandy distilled from morello cherries. Delicious drunk straight and excellent in a variety of food recipes.

Drambuie: A Scotch whisky liqueur. Made from a secret recipe dating back to 1745. "Dram Buidheach" the drink that satisfies.

Frangelico: A precious liqueur imported from Italy. Made from wild hazelnuts with infusions of berries and flowers to enrich the flavour.

Grand Marnier: An original blend of fine old Cognac and an extract of oranges. The recipe is over 150 years old

Kahlúa: A smooth, dark liqueur made from real coffee and fine clear spirits. Its origins are based in Mexico.

Lena Banana: Fresh ripe bananas are the perfect base for the definitive daiquiri and a host of other exciting fruit cocktails.

Malibu: A clear liqueur based on white rum with the subtle addition of coconut. Its distinctive taste blends naturally with virtually every mixer available.

Midori: Soft green, exudes freshness. Refreshing and mouthwatering honeydew melon. Simple yet complex. Smooth on the palate, serve on the rocks, or use to create summertime cocktails.

Ouzo – Aphrodite: The traditional spirit aperitif of Greece. The distinctive flavour is derived mainly from the seed of the anise plant. A neutral grain spirit, flavoured with anise and distilled in Australia.

Peach: The flavour of fresh peaches and natural peach juice make this cocktail lover's dream.

Peachtree Schnapps: Crystal clear, light liqueur, bursting with the taste of ripe peaches. Drink chilled or on the rocks or mix with any soft drink or juice.

Pineapple: A just ripe, sun-filled delight. Delicious neat, a necessity for summertime cocktails.

Rum – Bacardi: A smooth, dry, light bodied rum, especially suited for drinks in which you require subtle aroma and delicate flavour.

Rum – Bacardi Gold: Matured in charred oak barrels to give a dry smooth taste and a clear golden colour. Use in Bacardi drinks where you want a fuller, mellow flavour.

Rum – Bundaberg: The most popular Australian rum, mixes well with all juices and splits.

Rye Whiskey – Canadian Club: The largest selling Canadian Whiskey in North America and Australia. Distilled from corn, rye and malted barley. A light, mild and delicate Whiskey, ideal for drinking straight or in mixed cocktails.

Sabra: A unique flavour which comes from tangy jaffa oranges, with a hint of chocolate.

Sambuca – di Galliano: The Italian electric taste experience. Made from elderberries with a touch of anise.

Sambuca – Lago Nera: An exciting encounter between Sambuca di Galliano and extracts of black elderberry.

Sambuca – Opal Nera: The black Sambuca. Perfect after dinner or as an aperitif. The delicate oil from the Elderbush. The rich flavour of anise, with the subtle essence of lemon. Mingled, they are the dark secret of Opal Nera's delightful flavour.

Sambuca – Romana: The largest selling international Sambuca. It was the first ever produced and is fully imported from Italy.

Scotch Whisky – Ballantine's: One of the top three Scotch whiskies in the world. It is a blended whisky and is one of the very few "bottled in Scotland" products available in Australia.

Scotch Whisky – Johnnie Walker: Established 1820, distilled, blended and bottled in Scotland. Australia's largest selling Scotch whisky.

Southern Comfort: A liqueur not a bourbon as often thought. It is unique, full-bodied liquor with a touch of sweetness. Its recipe is a secret, but it is known to be based on peaches and apricots. It is the largest selling liqueur in Australia.

Strawberry: Fluorescent red, unmistakable strawberry bouquet. Natural liqueur delivers a true to nature, fresh strawberry flavour.

Tennessee Whiskey – Jack Daniel's: Contrary to popular belief, Jack Daniel's is not a bourbon, is a distinctive product called Tennessee Whiskey. Made from the 'old sour mash' process. Leached through hard maple charcoal, then aged in charred white oak barrels, at a controlled temperature, acquiring its body, bouquet and colour, yet remaining smooth.

Tequila – El Toro: A clear tequila imported from Mexico, with a scented clean character and slight burn, perfect for drinking straight, and is also a great mixer.

Tequila – Pepe Lopez: Distilled from the Mexcal variety of the agave plant – not Cacti. Pepe Lopez was named after a 19th Century Mexican bandit. A perfect mixer or drink straight with salt and lemon.

Tia Maria: A liqueur with a cane spirit base, and its flavour derived from the finest Jamaican coffee. It is not too sweet with a subtle taste of coffee.

Vandermint: A rich chocolate liqueur with the added zest of mint.

Vermouth: By description, Vermouth is a herbally infused wine. Three styles are most prevalent, these are:

Rosso: A bitter sweet herbal flavour, often drunk as an aperitif.

Bianco: Is light, fruity and refreshing. Mixes well with soda, lemonade and fruit juices.

Dry: Is crisp, light and dry and is used as a base for many cocktails.

Vodka - Smirnoff: The second largest selling spirit in the world and the leading Vodka in the world including Australia. Most Vodkas are steeped in tanks containing charcoal, but Smirnoff is pumped through ten columns of best hardwood charcoal for seven hours, removing all odours and impurities, making a superior quality product.

Shooters

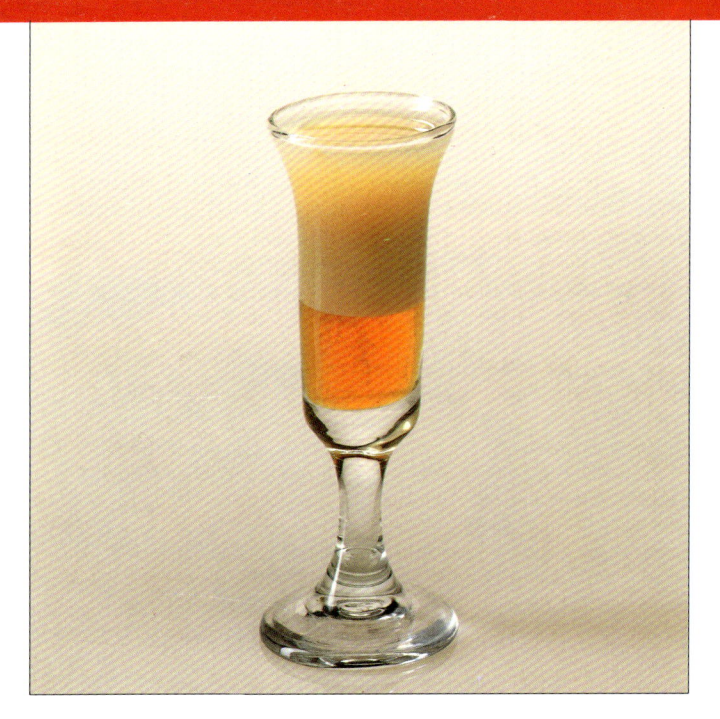

A.B.C.

Ingredients
Glass: Cordial (Embassy)
Mixers: 8ml Amaretto
10ml Baileys Irish Cream
12ml Cointreau

Method
Layer in order and shoot.

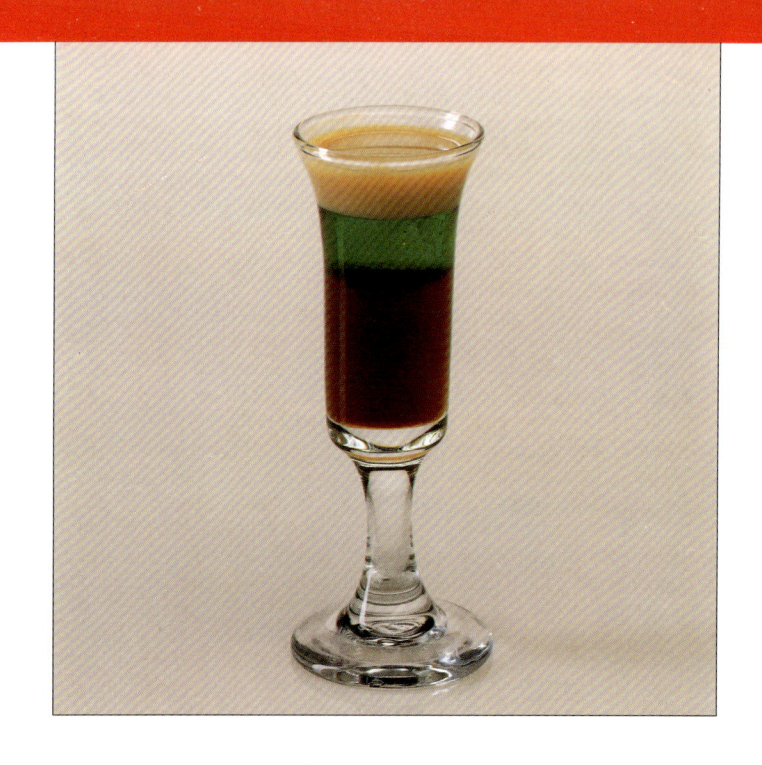

After Eight

Ingredients
Glass: Cordial (Embassy)
Mixers: 12ml Kahlúa
10ml Creme de Menthe
18ml Baileys Irish Cream

Method
Layer in order and shoot.

Shooters

Agent 99

Ingredients
Glass: Tall Dutch Cordial
Mixers: 15ml Parfait Amour
15ml Baileys Irish Cream
15ml Ouzo

Method
Layer in order and shoot.

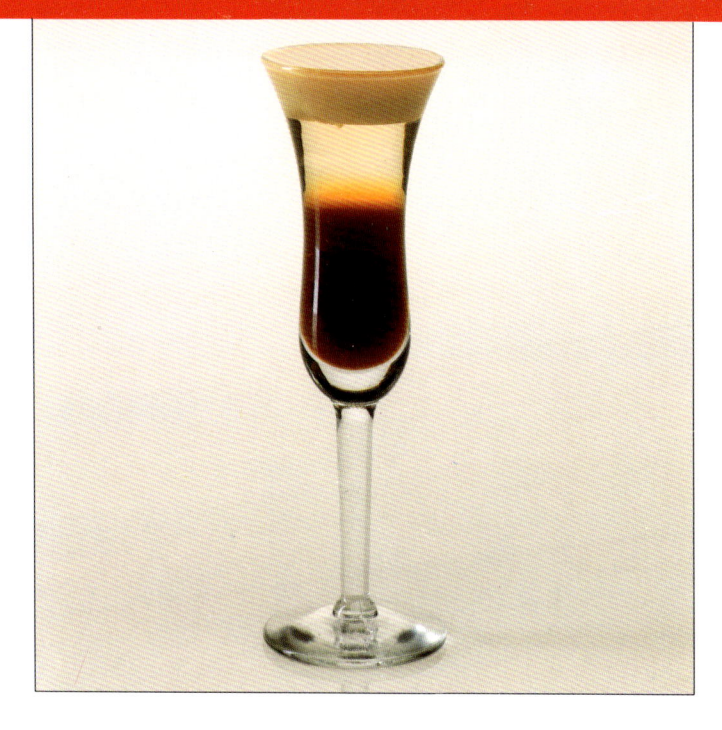

Altered State

Ingredients
Glass: Tall Dutch Cordial
Mixers: 15ml Kahlúa
15ml Peach Liqueur
15ml Baileys Irish Cream

Method
Layer in order and shoot.

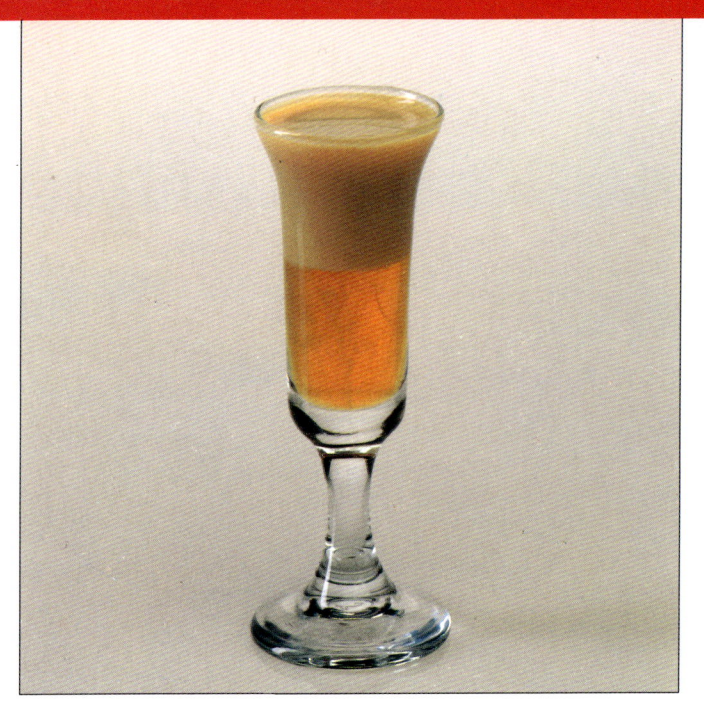

Shooters

Angel Dew
Ingredients
Glass: Cordial (Embassy)
Mixers: 15ml Benedictine
15ml Irish Cream

Method
Layer in order and shoot.

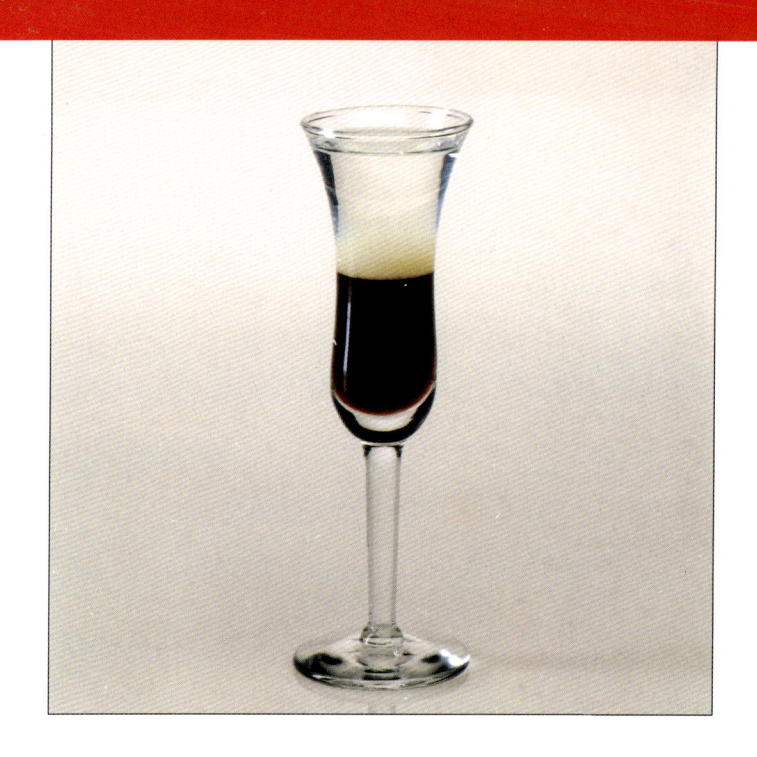

Angel Kiss
Ingredients
Glass: Tall Dutch Cordial
Mixers: 20ml Kahlúa
5ml Baileys Irish Cream
20ml Gin

Method
Layer in order and shoot.

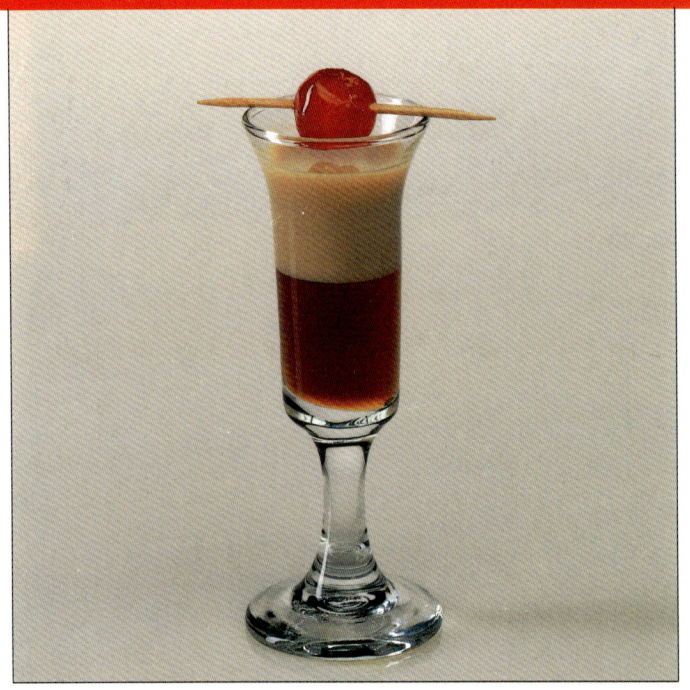

Shooters

Angel Tip
Ingredients
Glass: Cordial (Embassy)
Mixers: 15ml Creme de Cacao
              15ml Baileys Irish Cream
              cherry on a pick

Method
Layer in order, eat the cherry and shoot.

Angel Wing
Ingredients
Glass: Whisky Shot
Mixers: 15ml Creme de Cacao
              15ml Brandy
              15ml Baileys Irish Cream

Method
Layer in order and shoot.

Shooters

Atomic Bomb
Ingredients
Glass: Tall Dutch Cordial
Mixers: 20ml Tia Maria
15ml Gin
10ml cream

Method
Layer in order and shoot.

Avalanche
Ingredients
Glass: Cordial (Embassy)
Mixers: 10ml Kahlúa
8ml Dark Creme de Cacao
12ml Southern Comfort

Method
Layer in order and shoot.

Shooters

Banana Split
Ingredients
Glass: Tall Dutch Cordial
Mixers: 15ml Kahlúa
15ml Lena Banana Liqueur
10ml Strawberry Liqueur

Method
Layer in order and top with whipped cream. Shoot.

B.B.C.
Ingredients
Glass: Whisky Shot
Mixers: 15ml Benedictine
15ml Baileys Irish Cream
15ml Cointreau

Method
Layer in order and shoot.

Shooters

B.B.G.

Ingredients

Glass: Tall Dutch Cordial
Mixers: 15ml Benedictine
15ml Baileys Irish Cream
15ml Grand Marnier

Method
Layer in order and shoot.

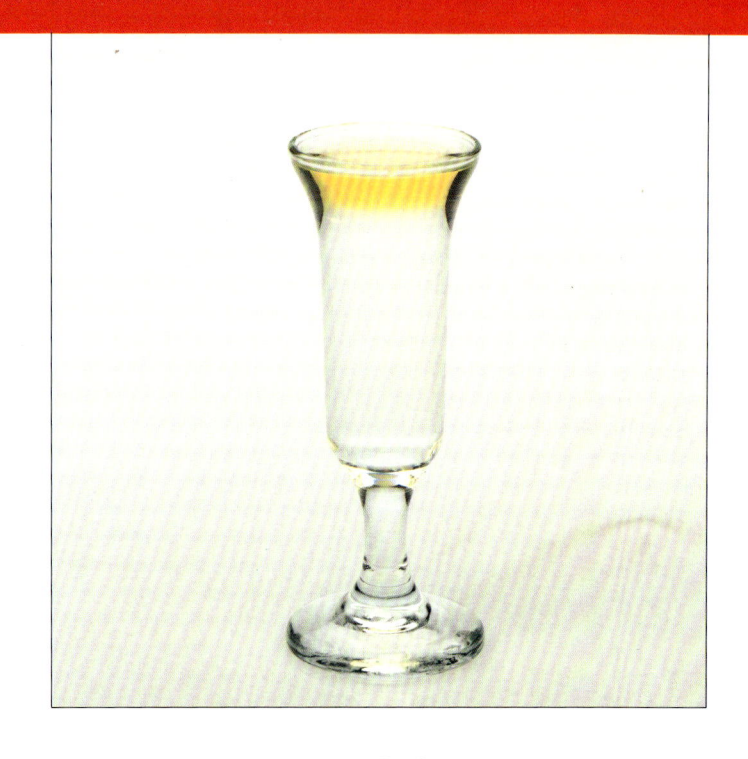

Bee Sting

Ingredients

Glass: Cordial (Embassy)
Mixers: 20ml Tequila
10ml Yellow Chartreuse

Method
Layer in order then light and shoot.

Shooters

B-53

Ingredients
Glass: Cordial (Embassy)
Mixers: 10ml Kahlúa
10ml Baileys Irish Cream
10ml Tequila

Method
Layer in order and shoot.

B-54

Ingredients
Glass: Whisky Shot
Mixers: 10ml Kahlúa
15ml Baileys Irish Cream
10ml Grand Marnier
10ml Tequila

Method
Layer in order and shoot.

Shooters

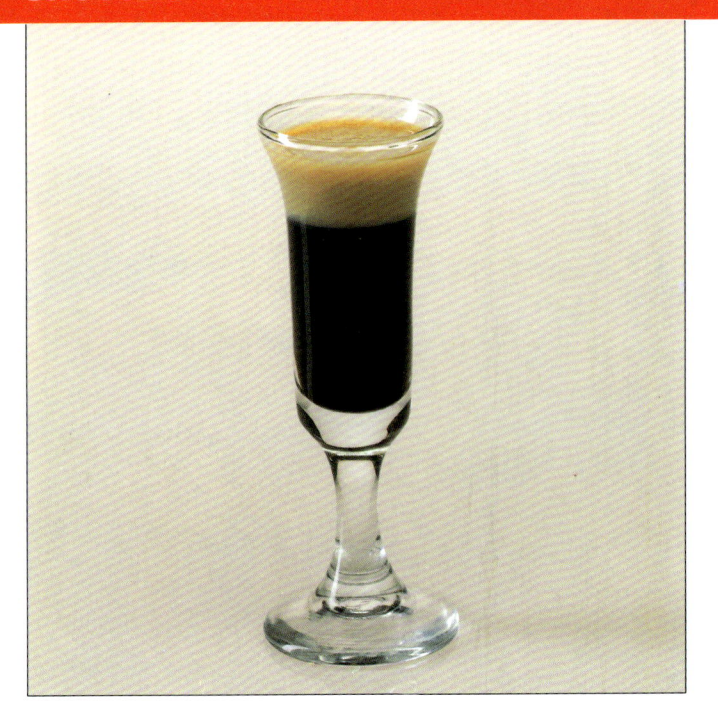

Black Dream

Ingredients
Glass: Cordial (Embassy)
Mixers: 20ml Opal Nera
10ml Baileys Irish Cream

Method
Layer in order and shoot.

Black Jack

Ingredients
Glass: Whisky Shot
Mixers: 20ml Kahlúa
25ml Ouzo

Method
Layer in order and shoot.

Shooters

Black Nuts
Ingredients
Glass: Cordial (Embassy)
Mixers: 15ml Opal Nera
15ml Frangelico

Method
Layer in order and shoot.

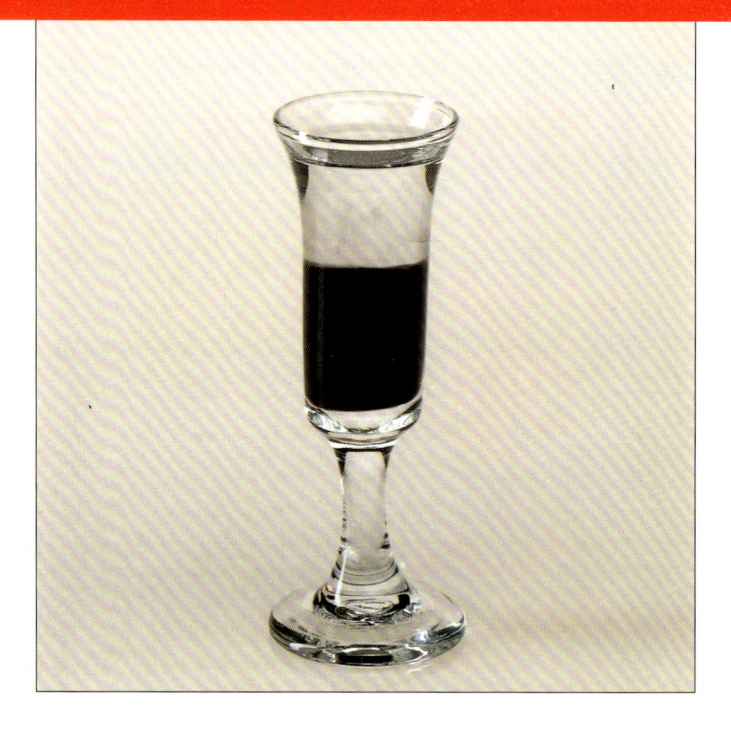

Black on White
Ingredients
Glass: Cordial (Embassy)
Mixers: 15ml Opal Nera
15ml White Sambuca

Method
Layer in order and shoot.

Shooters

Black Widow

Ingredients
Glass: Cordial (Embassy)
Mixers: 10ml Strawberry Liqueur
10ml Opal Nera
10ml cream

Method
Layer in order and shoot.

Blow Job

Ingredients
Glass: Tall Dutch Cordial
Mixers: 15ml Kahlúa
10ml Lena Banana Liqueur
15ml Baileys Irish Cream

Method
Layer in order and top with whipped cream. Shoot.

Shooters

Break

Ingredients
Glass: Cordial (Embassy)
Mixers: 10ml Kahlúa
         10ml Lena Banana Liqueur
         10ml Ouzo

Method
Layer in order and shoot.

Bull Shoot

Ingredients
Glass: Cordial (Embassy)
Mixers: 10ml Kahlúa
         10ml White Rum
         10ml Tequila

Method
Layer in order and shoot.

Shooters

Candy Cane

Ingredients
Glass: Tall Dutch Cordial
Mixers: 15ml Grenadine
         15ml Creme de Menthe
         15ml Vodka

Method
Layer in order and shoot.

Channel 64

Ingredients
Glass: Cordial (Embassy)
Mixers: 10ml Advocaat
         10ml Lena Banana Liqueur
         10ml Baileys Irish Cream

Method
Layer in order and shoot.

Shooters

Chastity Belt
Ingredients
Glass: Tall Dutch Cordial
Mixers: 20ml Tia Maria
10ml Frangelico
10ml Baileys Irish Cream
5ml cream

Method
Layer in order then float the cream. Shoot.

Chocolate Chip
Ingredients
Glass: Tall Dutch Cordial
Mixers: 15ml Vandermint
15ml Creme de Menthe
15ml Baileys Irish Cream

Method
Layer in order and shoot.

Shooters

Chocolate Nougat
Ingredients
Glass: Cordial (Embassy)
Mixers: 10ml Frangelico
10ml Baileys Irish Cream
10ml Yellow Chartreuse

Method
Layer in order and shoot.

Coathanger
Ingredients
Glass: Cordial (Lexington)
Mixers: 15ml Cointreau
15ml Tequila
7ml Grenadine or raspberry cordial
drop of milk

Method
Layer in order and shoot.

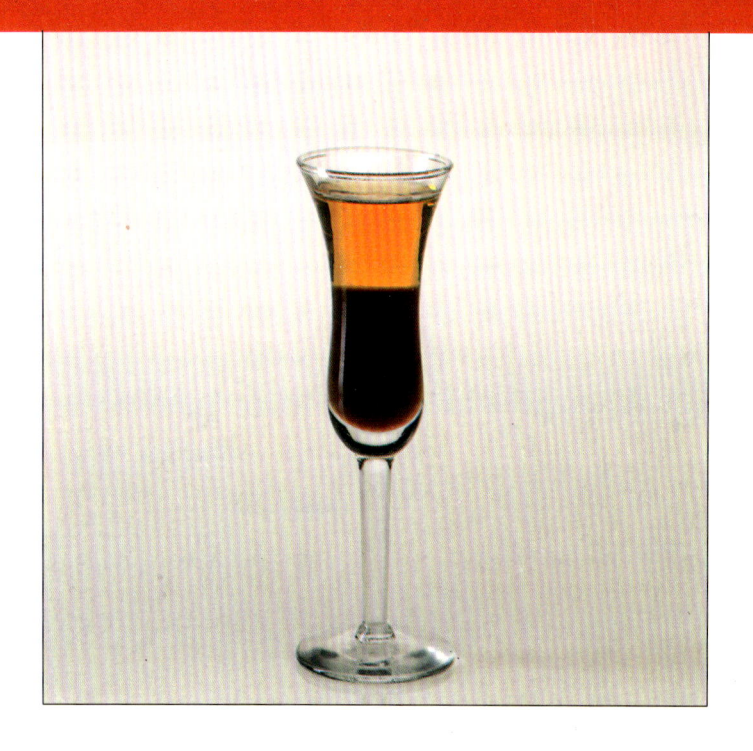

Shooters

Deep Throat
Ingredients
Glass: Tall Dutch Cordial
Mixers: 20ml Kahlúa
20ml Grand Marnier

Method
Layer in order and top with whipped cream. Shoot.

Devil's Handbrake
Ingredients
Glass: Tall Dutch Cordial
Mixers: 15ml Lena Banana Liqueur
15ml Mango Liqueur
15ml Cherry Brandy

Method
Layer in order and shoot.

Shooters

Eh-Bomb

Ingredients
Glass: Whisky Shot
Mixers: 10ml Creme de Menthe
10ml Baileys Irish Cream
10ml Ouzo
15ml Tequila

Method
Layer in order and shoot.

Electric Banana

Ingredients
Glass: Tall Dutch Cordial
Mixers: 15ml Lena Banana Liqueur
15ml lime juice
15ml Tequila

Method
Layer in order and shoot.

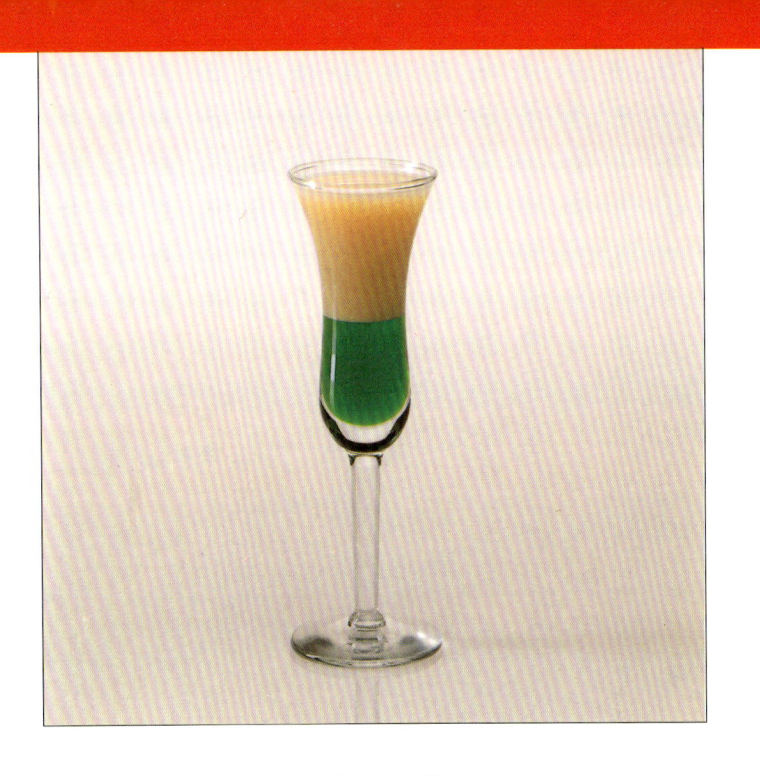

Shooters

El Revolto
Ingredients
Glass: Tall Dutch Cordial
Mixers: 15ml Creme de Menthe
15ml Baileys Irish Cream
15ml Cointreau

Method
Layer in order and shoot.

Face Off
Ingredients
Glass: Tall Dutch Cordial
Mixers: 10ml Grenadine
15ml Creme de Menthe
10ml Parfait Amour
10ml Sambuca

Method
Layer in order and shoot.

Shooters

Fire and Ice
Ingredients
Glass: Cordial (Embassy)
Mixers: 20ml Tequila
           10ml Creme de Menthe

Method
Layer in order and shoot.

Flame Thrower
Ingredients
Glass: Tall Dutch Cordial
Mixers: 20ml Dark Creme de Cacao
           25ml B & B

Method
Layer in order and shoot.

Shooters

Flaming Diamond
Ingredients
Glass: Cordial (Embassy)
Mixers: 10ml Strawberry Liqueur
10ml Grand Marnier
10ml Vodka

Method
Layer in order and shoot.

Flaming Orgy
Ingredients
Glass: Tall Dutch Cordial
Mixers: 10ml Grenadine
10ml Creme de Menthe
15ml Brandy
10ml Tequila

Method
Layer in order and shoot.

Shooters

401

Ingredients

Glass: Cordial (Embassy)
Mixers: 10ml Kahlúa
             10ml Lena Banana Liqueur
             5ml Baileys Irish Cream
             5ml Jack Daniel's Tennessee Whiskey

Method

Layer in order and shoot.

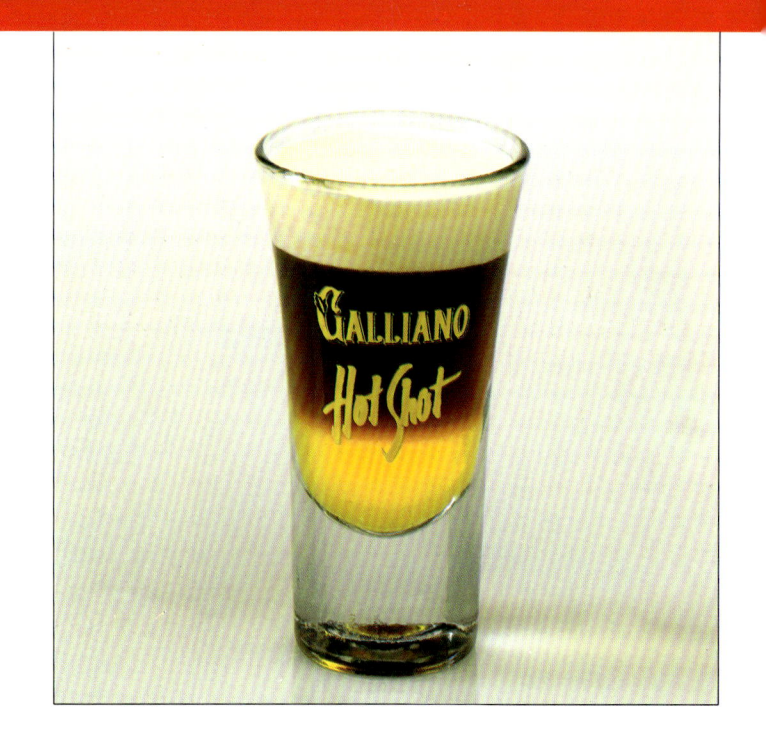

Galliano Hot Shot

Ingredients

Glass: Galliano Hot Shot Glass
Mixers: 15ml Galliano
             25ml black coffee
             5ml cream

Method

Top Galliano with black coffee, then float cream. Shoot.

Shooters

Ghetto Blaster
Ingredients
Glass: Whisky Shot
Mixers: 10ml Kahlúa
            25ml Tequila
            10ml Rye Whiskey

Method
Layer in order and shoot.

Godfather
Ingredients
Glass: Cordial (Embassy)
Mixers: 15ml Amaretto
            15ml Scotch Whisky

Method
Layer in order and shoot.

Shooters

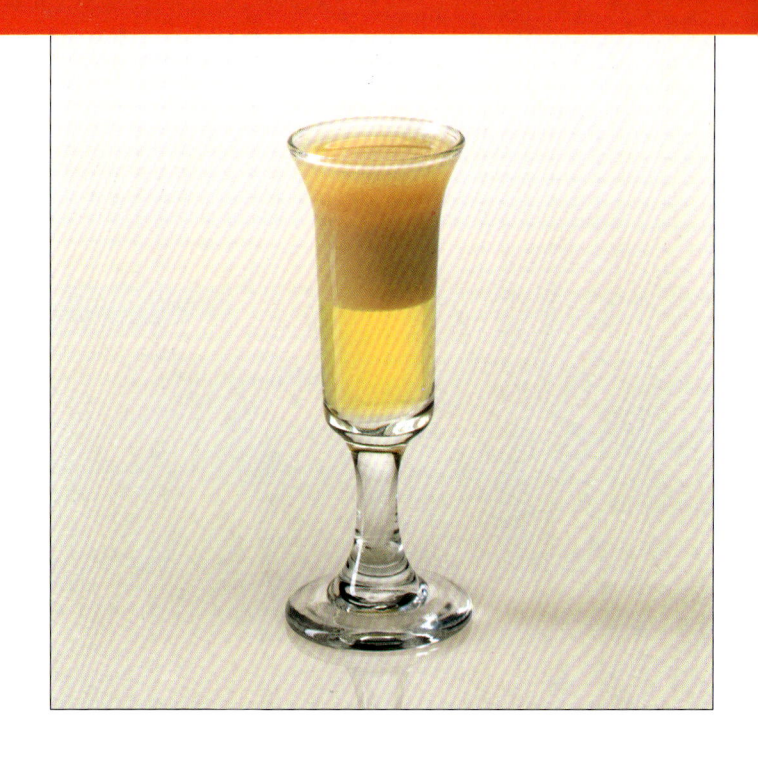

Grand Baileys
Ingredients
Glass: Cordial (Embassy)
Mixers: 20ml Baileys Irish Cream
10ml Grand Marnier

Method
Layer in order and shoot.

Grand Slam
Ingredients
Glass: Cordial (Embassy)
Mixers: 10ml Lena Banana Liqueur
10ml Baileys Irish Cream
10ml Grand Marnier

Method
Layer in order and shoot.

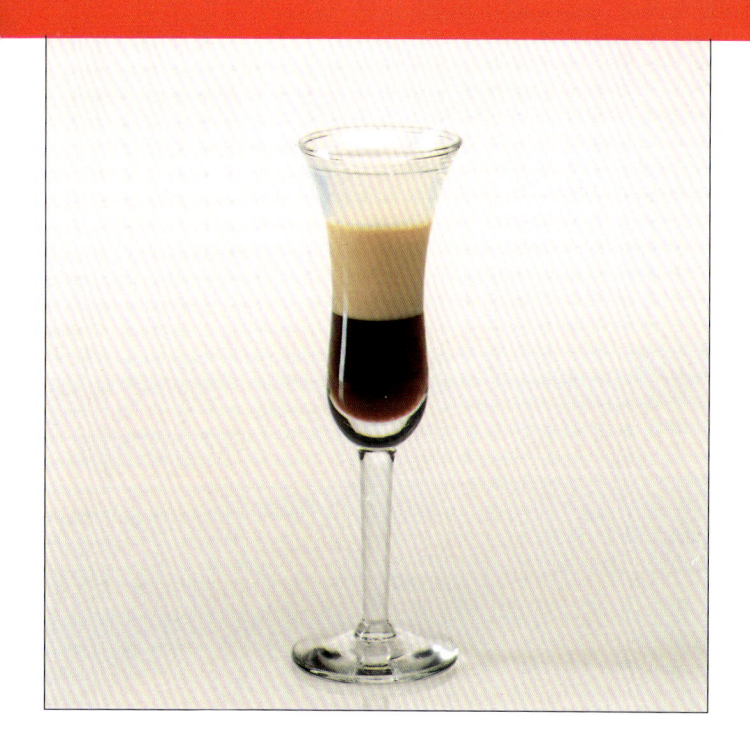

Shooters

Great White North
Ingredients
Glass: Tall Dutch Cordial
Mixers: 15ml Kahlúa
15ml Baileys Irish Cream
15ml Ouzo

Method
Layer in order and shoot.

Green Devil
Ingredients
Glass: Whisky Shot
Mixers: 25ml Dark Rum
20ml Creme de Menthe

Method
Layer in order and shoot.

Shooters

Harbour Lights
Ingredients
Glass: Cordial (Lexington)
Mixers: 12ml Kahlúa
12ml Sambuca
12ml Green Chartreuse

Method
Layer in order and straw shoot.

Hard On
Ingredients
Glass: Cordial (Lexington)
Mixers: 12ml Kahlúa
12ml Amaretto
13ml Baileys Irish Cream

Method
Layer in order and shoot.

Shooters

Hellraiser

Ingredients
Glass: Whisky Shot
Mixers: 15ml Midori
15ml Strawberry Liqueur
15ml Opal Nera

Method
Layer in order and shoot.

Horney Bull

Ingredients
Glass: Cordial (Embassy)
Mixers: 10ml Vodka
10ml Rum
10ml Tequila

Method
Layer in order and shoot.

Shooters

Irish Flag

Ingredients
Glass: Cordial (Lexington)
Mixers: 12ml Green Creme de Menthe
          12ml Baileys Irish Cream
          12ml Brandy

Method
Layer in order and shoot.

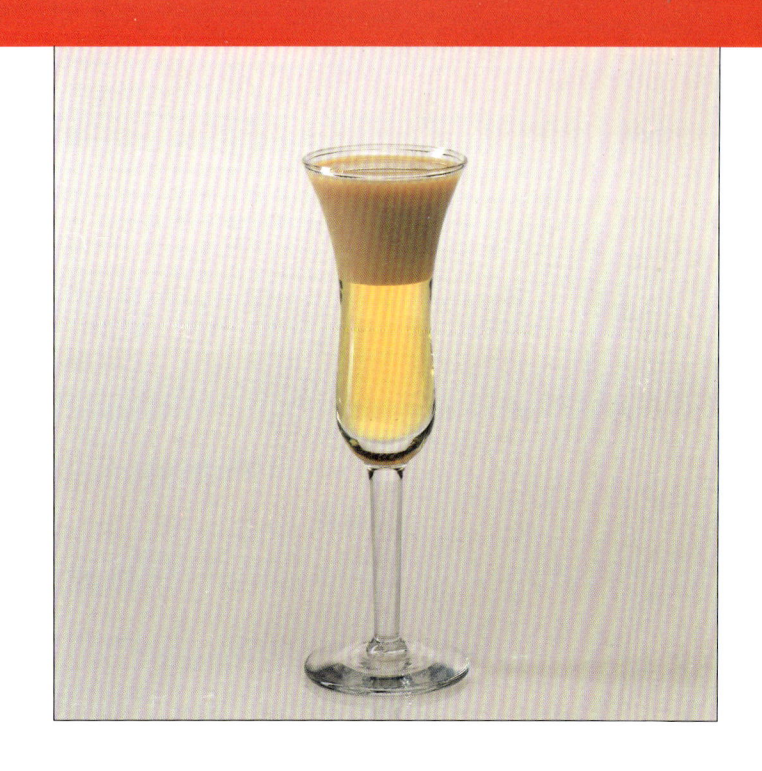

Irish Monkey

Ingredients
Glass: Tall Dutch Cordial
Mixers: 20ml Lena Banana Liqueur
          25ml Baileys Irish Cream

Method
Layer in order and shoot.

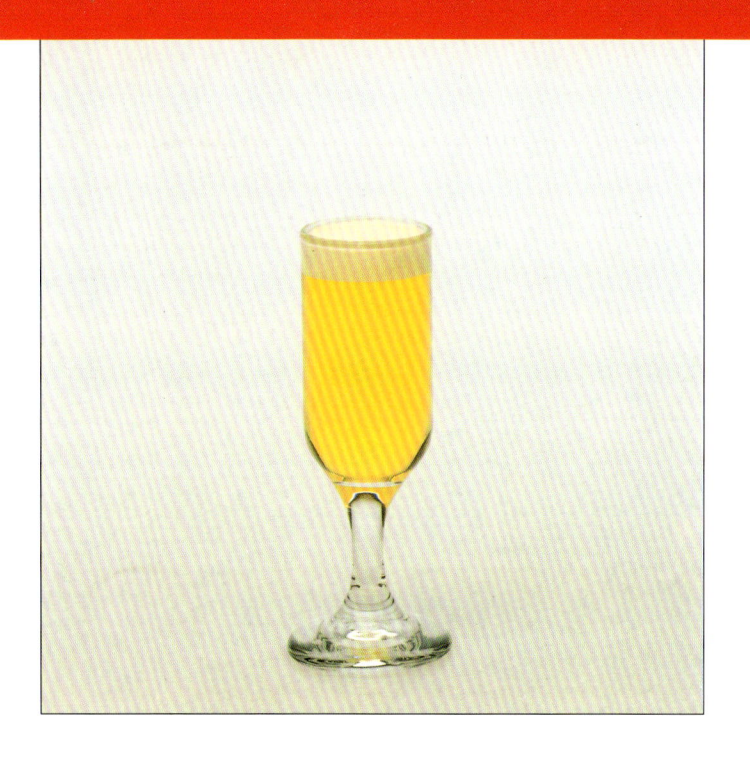

Shooters

Italian Stallion
Ingredients
Glass: Cordial (Lexington)
Mixers: 10ml Lena Banana Liqueur
10ml Galliano
17ml cream

Method
Layer in order and shoot.

Jane's Touch
Ingredients
Glass: Cordial (Embassy)
Mixers: 10ml Kahlúa
10ml Frangelico
10ml Baileys Irish Cream

Method
Layer in order and shoot.

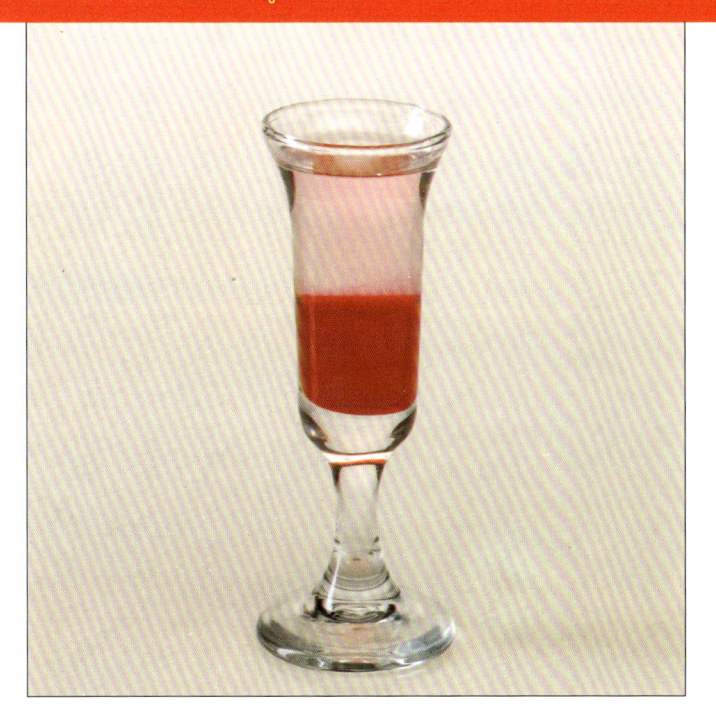

Shooters

Jelly Bean
INGREDIENTS
Glass: Cordial (Embassy)
Mixers: 10ml Grenadine
10ml Ouzo
10ml Tequila

Method
Layer in order and shoot.

Kamikaze
INGREDIENTS
Glass: Whisky Shot
Mixers: 22ml Cointreau
22ml Vodka
5ml Berri Lemon Juice

Method
Layer in order and shoot.

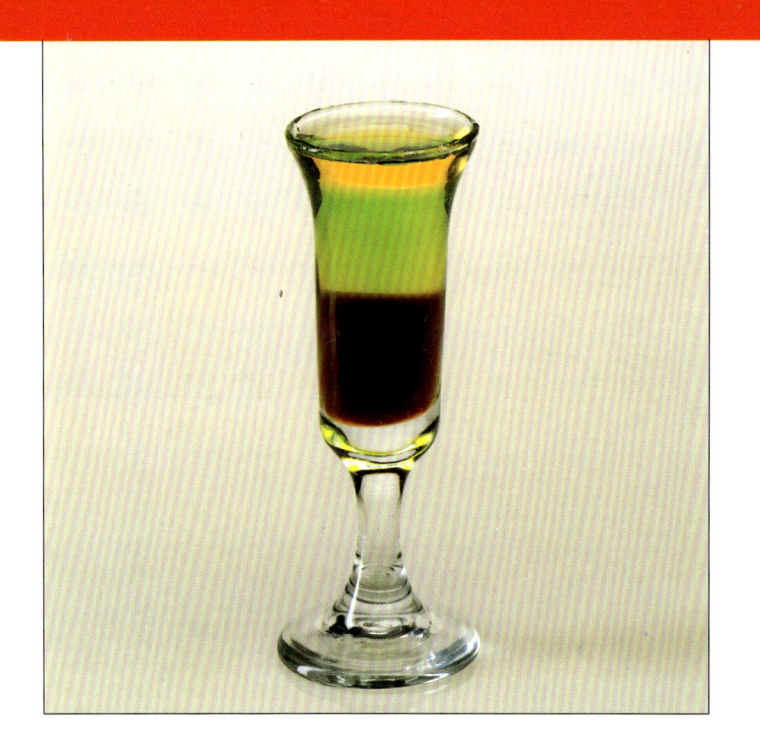

Shooters

Lady Killer
Ingredients
Glass: Cordial (Embassy)
Mixers: 15ml Kahlúa
         10ml Midori
         5ml Frangelico

Method
Layer in order and shoot.

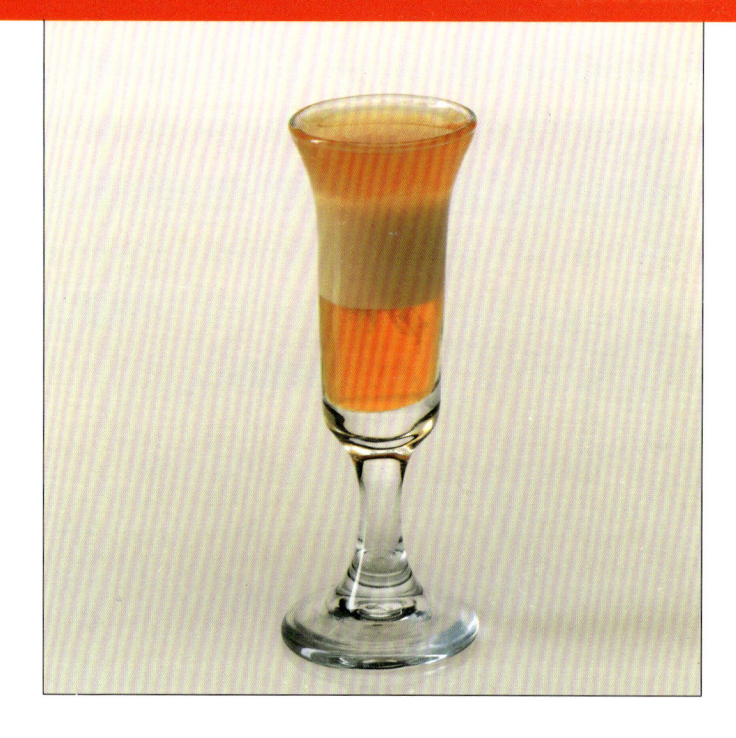

Landslider
Ingredients
Glass: Cordial (Embassy)
Mixers: 10ml Amaretto
         10ml Baileys Irish Cream
         10ml Grand Marnier

Method
Layer in order and shoot.

Shooters

Laser Beam
Ingredients
Glass: Tall Dutch Cordial
Mixers: 25ml Galliano
20ml Tequila

Method
Layer in order and shoot.

Leather and Lace
Ingredients
Glass: Cordial (Embassy)
Mixers: 10ml Kahlúa
10ml Vodka
10ml Baileys Irish Cream

Method
Layer in order and shoot.

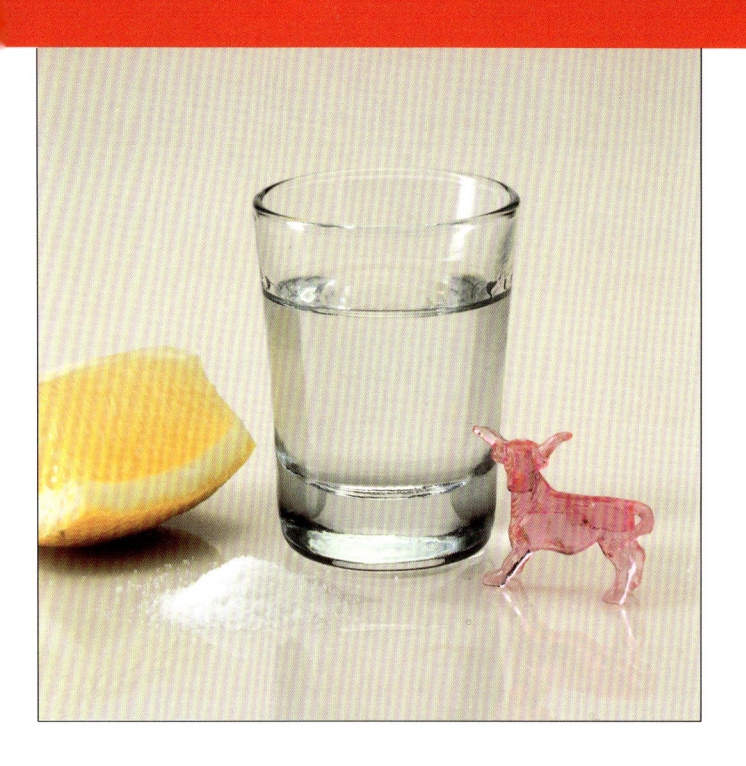

Shooters

Lick Sip Suck
Ingredients
Glass: Whisky Shot
Mixers: 30ml Tequila
lemon in quarters or slices
salt

Method
Pour Tequila into glass. On the flat piece of skin between the base of your thumb and index finger, place a pinch of salt. Place a quarter of the lemon by you on the bar. Lick the salt off your hand, shoot the Tequila and then suck the lemon in quick succession.

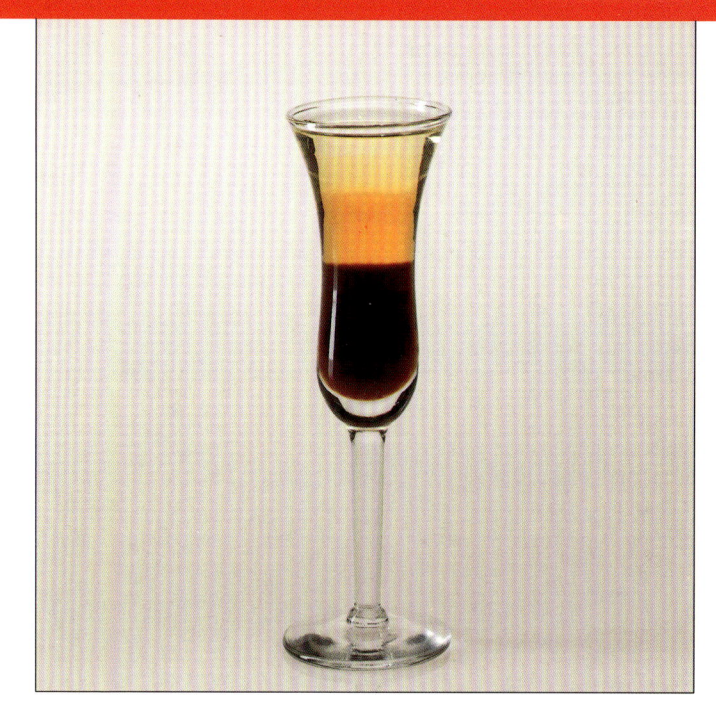

Light House
Ingredients
Glass: Tall Dutch Cordial
Mixers: 15ml Kahlúa
15ml Grand Marnier
15ml Tequila

Method
Layer in order and shoot.

Shooters

Lone Star
Ingredients
Glass: Cordial (Embassy)
Mixers: 15ml Cherry Brandy
10ml Parfait Amour
5ml Bacardi

Method
Layer in order and shoot.

Mexican Berry
Ingredients
Glass: Cordial (Embassy)
Mixers: 10ml Kahlúa
10ml Strawberry Liqueur
10ml Tequila

Method
Layer in order and shoot.

Shooters

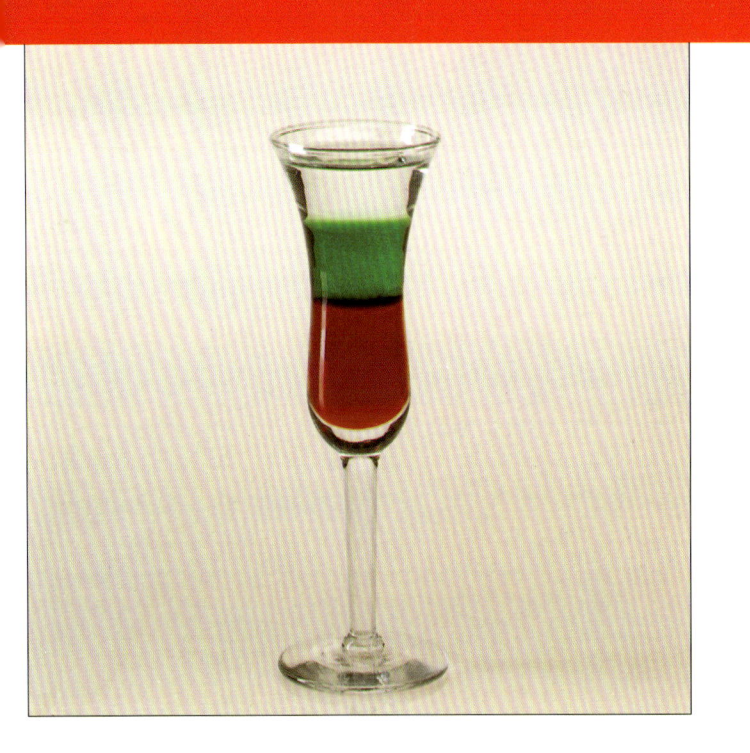

Mexican Flag
Ingredients
Glass: Tall Dutch Cordial
Mixers: 15ml Grenadine
15ml Creme de Menthe
15ml Tequila

Method
Layer in order and shoot.

Mexican Pumper
Ingredients
Glass: Cordial (Lexington)
Mixers: 12ml Grenadine
12ml Kahlúa
12ml Tequila

Method
Layer in order and shoot.

Shooters

Miles of Smiles
Ingredients
Glass: Tall Dutch Cordial
Mixers: 15ml Creme de Menthe
15ml Amaretto
15ml Rye Whiskey

Method
Layer in order and shoot.

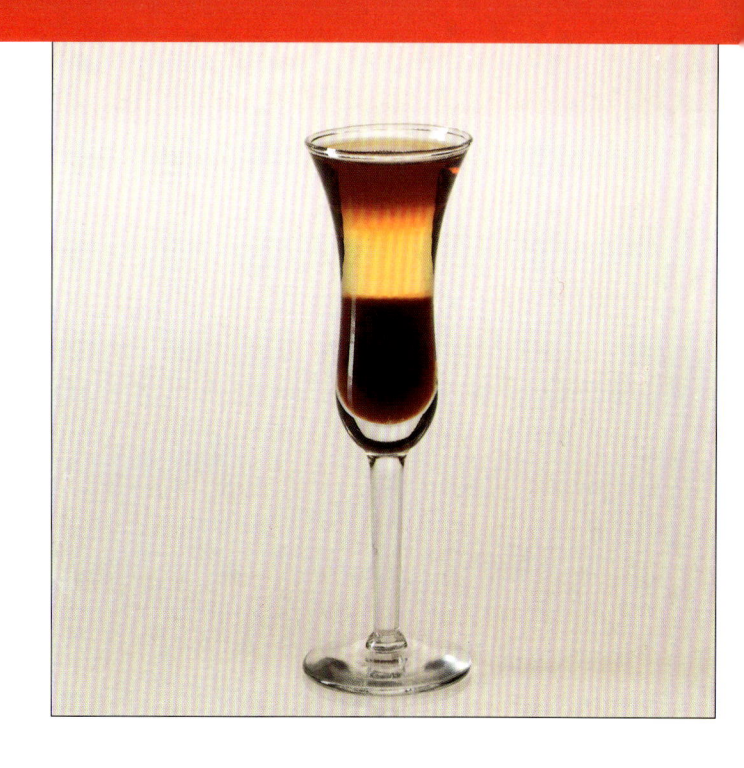

Model "T"
Ingredients
Glass: Tall Dutch Cordial
Mixers: 15ml Kahlúa
15ml Lena Banana Liqueur
15ml Tia Maria

Method
Layer in order and shoot.

Shooters

Monkey's Punch
Ingredients
Glass: Cordial (Lexington)
Mixers: 10ml Kahlúa
15ml Creme de Menthe
15ml Baileys Irish Cream

Method
Layer in order and shoot.

Neutron Bomb
Ingredients
Glass: Whisky Shot
Mixers: 15ml Kahlúa
15ml Bundaberg Rum
15ml Tequila

Method
Layer in order and shoot.

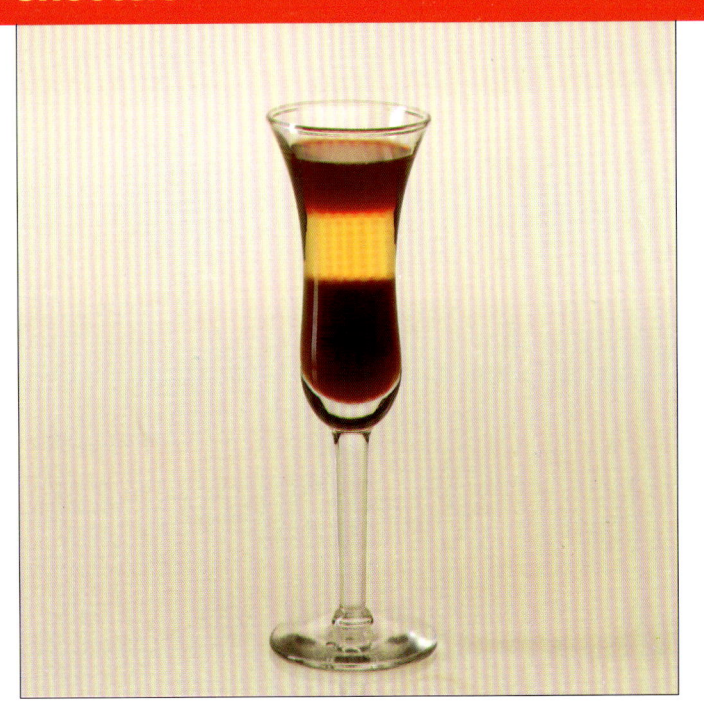

Shooters

19 Duke Drive
Ingredients
Glass: Tall Dutch Cordial
Mixers: 15ml Vandermint
         15ml Cherry Brandy
         15ml Lena Banana Liqueur

Method
Layer in order and shoot.

Nude Bomb
Ingredients
Glass: Cordial (Embassy)
Mixers: 10ml Kahlúa
         10ml Amaretto
         10ml Lena Banana Liqueur

Method
Layer in order and shoot.

Shooters

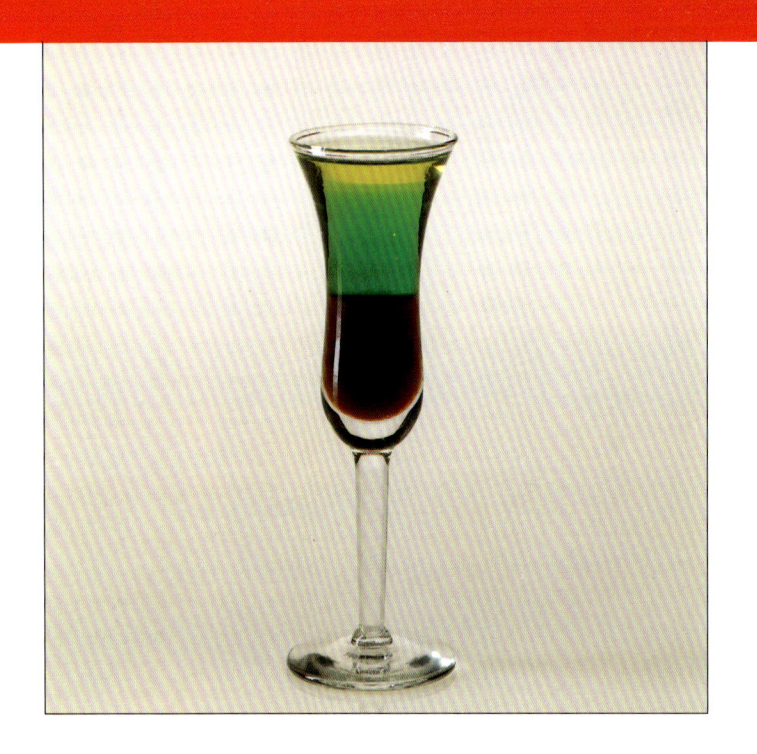

Nutty Buddy
Ingredients
Glass: Tall Dutch Cordial
Mixers: 15ml Kahlúa
15ml Creme de Menthe
15ml Frangelico

Method
Layer in order and shoot.

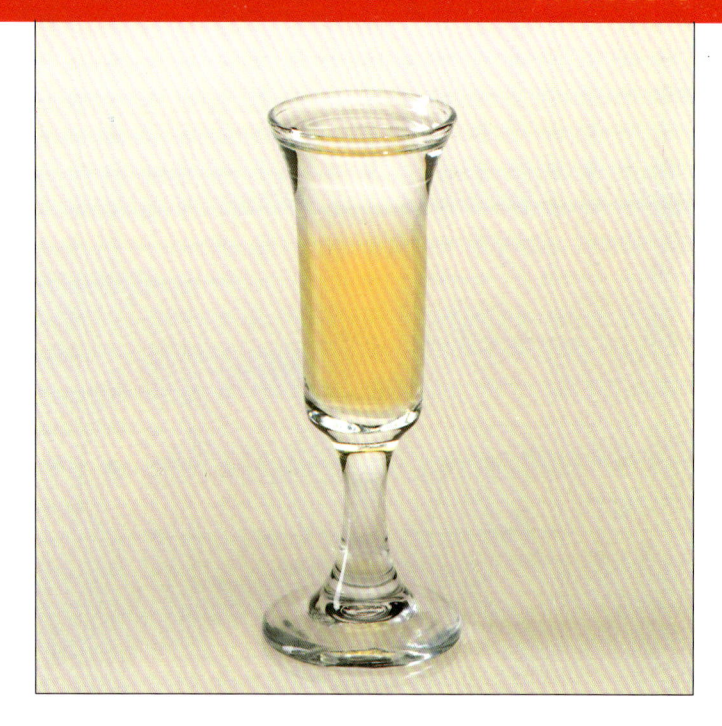

Panty Dropper
Ingredients
Glass: Cordial (Embassy)
Mixers: 20ml Frangelico
10ml Gin

Method
Layer in order and shoot.

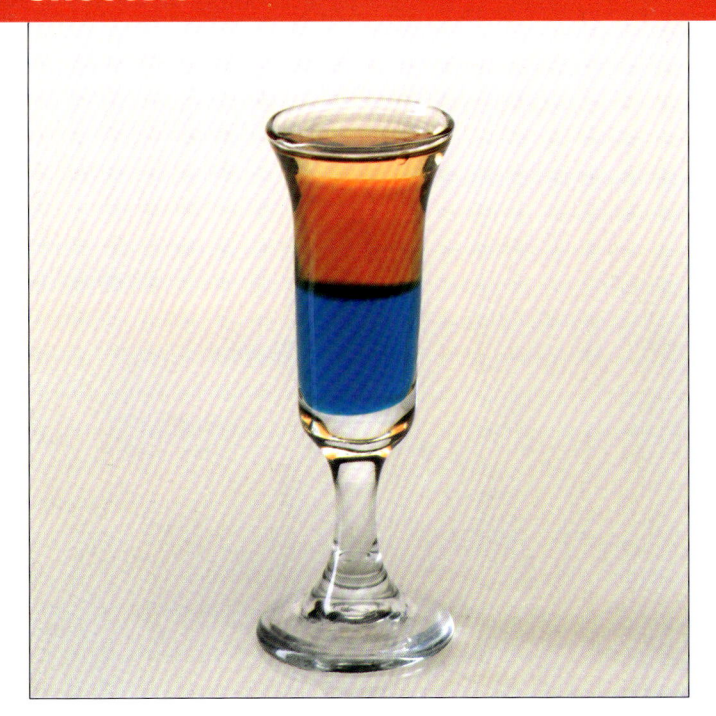

Shooters

Okanagan
Ingredients
Glass: Cordial (Embassy)
Mixers: 10ml Blue Curacao
15ml Strawberry Liqueur
5ml Coconut Liqueur

Method
Layer in order and shoot.

Penalty Shot
Ingredients
Glass: Whisky Shot
Mixers: 15ml Creme de Menthe
15ml Tia Maria
15ml Vodka

Method
Layer in order and shoot.

Shooters

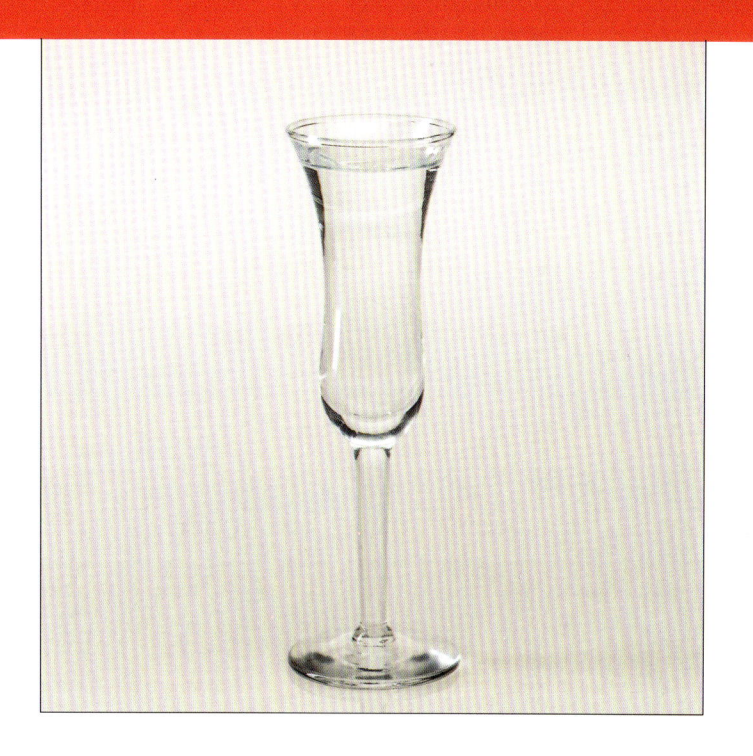

Pipeline

Ingredients

Glass: Tall Dutch Cordial
Mixers: 25ml Tequila
20ml Vodka

Method

Layer in order and shoot.

Popsicle

Ingredients

Glass: Cordial (Lexington)
Mixers: 15ml Tia Maria
10ml Baileys Irish Cream
15ml Vodka

Method

Layer in order and shoot.

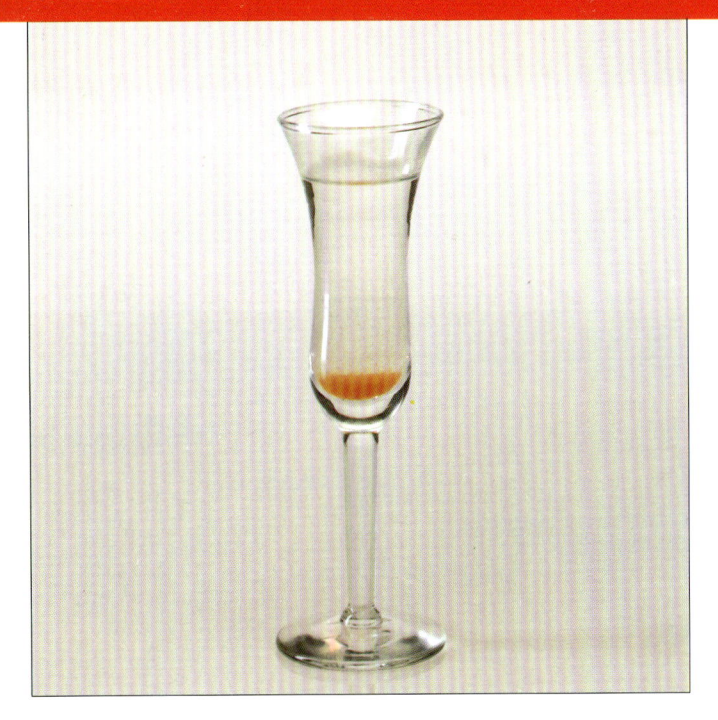

Shooters

Prairie Fire
Ingredients
Glass: Tall Dutch Cordial
Mixers: 45ml Tequila
10 drops Tabasco Sauce

Method
Layer in order and shoot.

Quicksilver
Ingredients
Glass: Cordial (Embassy)
Mixers: 10ml Lena Banana Liqueur
10ml Tequila
10ml Vodka

Method
Layer in order and shoot.

Shooters

Raider

Ingredients
Glass: Whisky Shot
Mixers: 15ml Baileys Irish Cream
15ml Grand Marnier
15ml Cointreau

Method
Layer in order and shoot.

Ready, Set, Go!

Ingredients
Glass: Tall Dutch Cordial
Mixers: 15ml Strawberry Liqueur
15ml Lena Banana Liqueur
15ml Midori

Method
Layer in order and straw shoot.

Shooters

Ryan's Rush

Ingredients
Glass: Cordial (Embassy)
Mixers: 10ml Kahlúa
10ml Baileys Irish Cream
10ml Bacardi

Method
Layer in order and shoot.

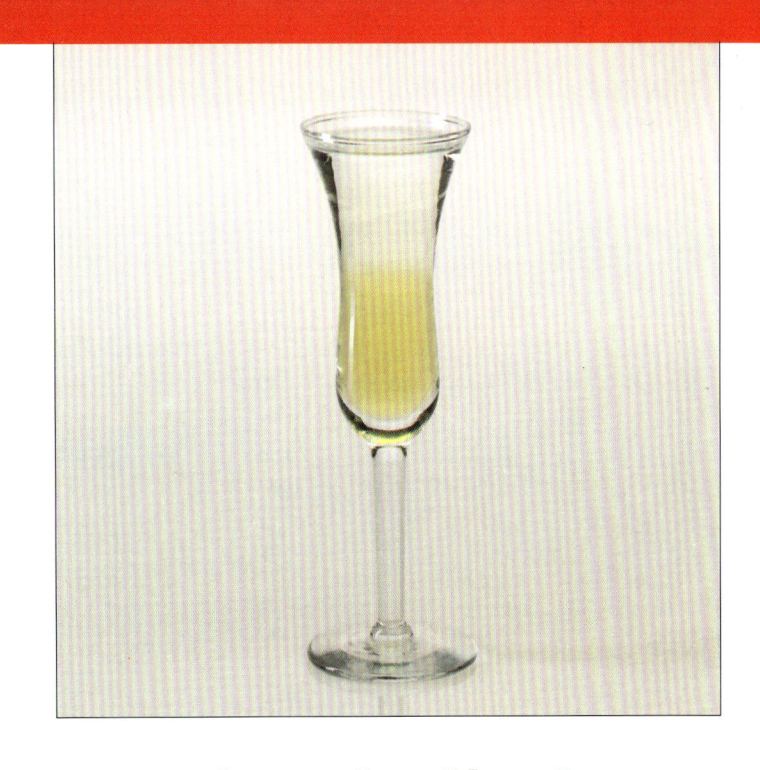

Screaming Lizard

Ingredients
Glass: Tall Dutch Cordial
Mixers: 25ml Tequila
20ml Green Chartreuse

Method
Layer in order and shoot.

Shooters

Seduction
Ingredients
Glass: Cordial (Lexington)
Mixers: 12ml Lena Banana Liqueur
12ml Frangelico
12ml Baileys Irish Cream

Method
Layer in order and shoot.

Shamrock
Ingredients
Glass: Cordial (Embassy)
Mixers: 10ml Creme de Cacao
10ml Creme de Menthe
10ml Baileys Irish Cream

Method
Layer in order and shoot.

Shooters

Silver Thread
Ingredients
Glass: Tall Dutch Cordial
Mixers: 15ml Creme de Menthe
15ml Lena Banana Liqueur
15ml Tia Maria

Method
Layer in order and shoot.

69er
Ingredients
Glass: Whisky Shot
Mixers: 15ml Lena Banana Liqueur
15ml Baileys Irish Cream
15ml Ouzo

Method
Layer in order and shoot.

Slippery Nipple

Ingredients
Glass: Tall Dutch Cordial
Mixers: 30ml Sambuca
15ml Baileys Irish Cream

Method
Layer in order and shoot.

Smartie

Ingredients
Glass: Cordial (Embassy)
Mixers: 15ml Grenadine
10ml Kahlúa
5ml Tequila

Method
Layer in order and shoot.

Shooters

Snake Bite

Ingredients
Glass: Whisky Shot
Mixers: 25ml Tequila
           20ml Creme de Menthe

Method
Layer in order and shoot.

Test Tube Baby

Ingredients
Glass: Tall Dutch Cordial
Mixers: 25ml Grand Marnier
           20ml Ouzo
           drop of Baileys Irish Cream

Method
Layer in order and shoot.

T.K.O.

Ingredients
Glass: Cordial (Embassy)
Mixers: 10ml Kahlúa
10ml Tequila
10ml Ouzo

Method
Layer in order and shoot.

Traffic Light

Ingredients
Glass: Tall Dutch Cordial
Mixers: 10ml Strawberry Liqueur
10ml Galliano
25ml Green Chartreuse

Method
Layer in order, light, then straw shoot.

Shooters

Vibrator
Ingredients
Glass: Cordial (Embassy)
Mixers: 10ml Baileys Irish Cream
20ml Southern Comfort

Method
Layer in order and shoot.

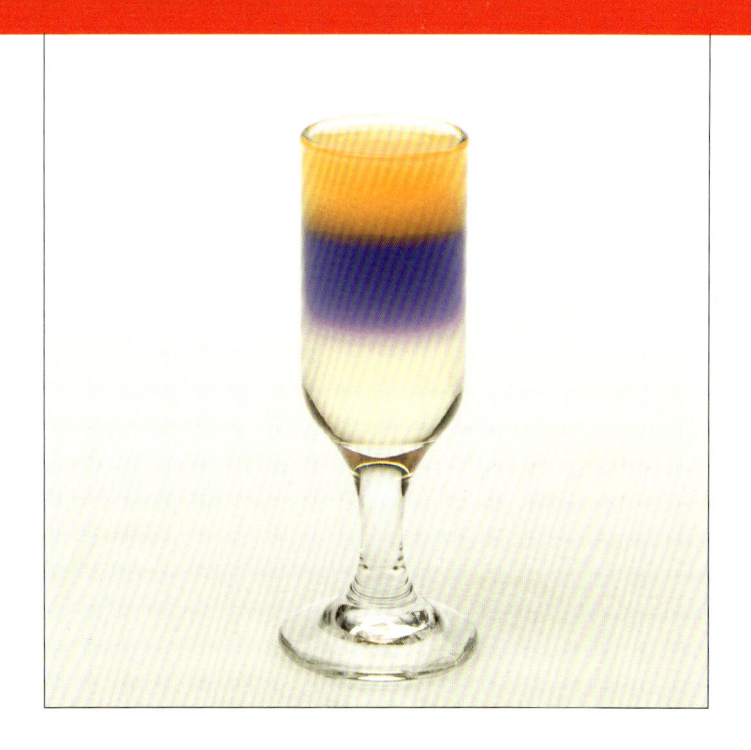

Violet Slumber
Ingredients
Glass: Cordial (Lexington)
Mixers: 15ml Malibu
12ml Parfait Amour
10ml Berri Orange Juice

Method
Layer in order and shoot.

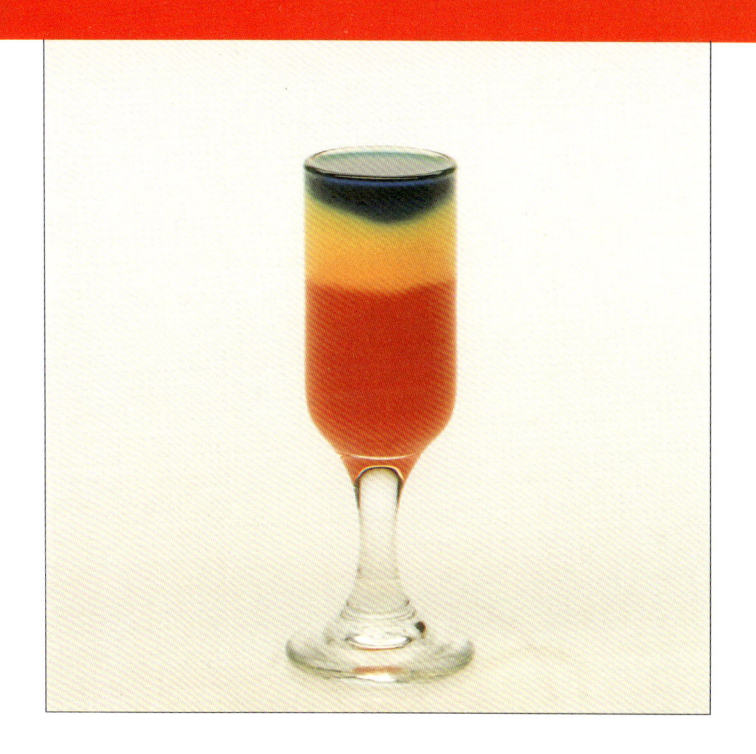

Shooters

Water-Bubba
Ingredients
Glass: Cordial (Lexington)
Mixers: 15ml Cherry Advocaat
         10ml Advocaat
         12ml Blue Curacao

Method
Pour Advocaat into Cherry Advocaat, then layer the Blue Curacao and shoot.

Zipper
Ingredients
Glass: Whisky Shot
Mixers: 15ml Tequila
         15ml Baileys Irish Cream
         15ml Grand Marnier

Method
Layer in order and shoot.

Shooters Index

A.B.C. ... 6	El Revolto ... 23	Mexican Pumper ... 39
After Eight ... 6	Face Off ... 23	Miles of Smiles ... 40
Agent 99 ... 7	Fire and Ice ... 24	Model "T" ... 40
Altered State ... 7	Flame Thrower ... 24	Monkey's Punch ... 41
Angel Dew ... 8	Flaming Diamond ... 25	Neutron Bomb ... 41
Angel Kiss ... 8	Flaming Orgy ... 25	19 Duke Drive ... 42
Angel Tip ... 9	401 ... 26	Nude Bomb ... 42
Angel Wing ... 9	Galliano Hot Shot ... 26	Nutty Buddy ... 43
Atomic Bomb ... 10	Ghetto Blaster ... 27	Panty Dropper ... 43
Avalanche ... 10	Godfather ... 27	Okanagan ... 44
Banana Split ... 11	Grand Baileys ... 28	Penalty Shot ... 44
B.B.C. ... 11	Grand Slam ... 28	Pipeline ... 45
B.B.G. ... 12	Great White North ... 29	Popsicle ... 45
Bee Sting ... 12	Green Devil ... 29	Prairie Fire ... 46
B-53 ... 13	Harbour Lights ... 30	Quicksilver ... 46
B-54 ... 13	Hard On ... 30	Raider ... 47
Black Dream ... 14	Hellraiser ... 31	Ready, Set, Go! ... 47
Black Jack ... 14	Horney Bull ... 31	Ryan's Rush ... 48
Black Nuts ... 15	Irish Flag ... 32	Screaming Lizard ... 48
Black on White ... 15	Irish Monkey ... 32	Seduction ... 49
Black Widow ... 16	Italian Stallion ... 33	Shamrock ... 49
Blow Job ... 16	Jane's Touch ... 33	Silver Thread ... 50
Break ... 17	Jelly Bean ... 34	69er ... 50
Bull Shoot ... 17	Kamikaze ... 34	Slippery Nipple ... 51
Candy Cane ... 18	Lady Killer ... 35	Smartie ... 51
Channel 64 ... 18	Landslider ... 35	Snake Bite ... 52
Chastity Belt ... 19	Laser Beam ... 36	Test Tube Baby ... 52
Chocolate Chip ... 19	Leather and Lace ... 36	T.K.O. ... 53
Chocolate Nougat ... 20	Lick Sip Suck ... 37	Traffic Light ... 53
Coathanger ... 20	Light House ... 37	Vibrator ... 54
Deep Throat ... 21	Lone Star ... 38	Violet Slumber ... 54
Devil's Handbrake ... 21	Mexican Berry ... 38	Water-Bubba ... 55
Eh-Bomb ... 22	Mexican Flag ... 39	Zipper ... 55
Electric Banana ... 22		